Deserts

By Christy Steele

Steadwell Books

Raintree Steck-Vaughn Publishers
A Harcourt Company

Austin · New York
www.steck-vaughn.com

Published by Raintree Steck-Vaughn Publishers, an imprint of Steck-Vaughn Company.

Library of Congress Cataloging-in-Publication Data
Cataloging-in-Publication data is available upon request.

Produced by Compass Books

Photo Acknowledgments
Corbis/Andrew Brown, 4; Craig Aurness, 10; Gorden Whitten, 12; Wolfgang Kaehler, 14; George Lepp, 16; Buddy Mays, 18; Mary Ann McDonald, 20; David Cumming; Eye Ubiquitous, 26; Kevin Schafer, 28, Digital Stock Photos, title page, 22, 25 Photo Network/Henry T. Kaiser, cover

Content Consultants
Susan L. Woodward
Professor of Geography
Radford University
Radford, Virginia

Maria Kent Rowell
Science Consultant
Sebastopol, California

David Larwa
National Science Education Consultant
Educational Training Services
Brighton, Michigan

CONTENTS

These cactus plants have adapted to grow in the desert biome.

THE DESERT BIOME

Some scientists study parts of Earth called biomes. Biomes are large regions, or areas, that have communities of plants and animals. A community is a group of plants and animals that live in the same place. Deserts are a biome.

Each biome has a different **climate**. Climate is the usual weather in a place. Climate includes wind speeds, amount of rainfall, and temperature. Temperature measures how hot or cold a place is.

Different biomes have different kinds of soils. Many kinds of plants grow in biomes with rich soil. Fewer plants grow in biomes with dry, poor, or wind-blown soil.

Plants and animals are **adapted** to their biomes. To be adapted means that a living thing has features that help it fit where it lives.

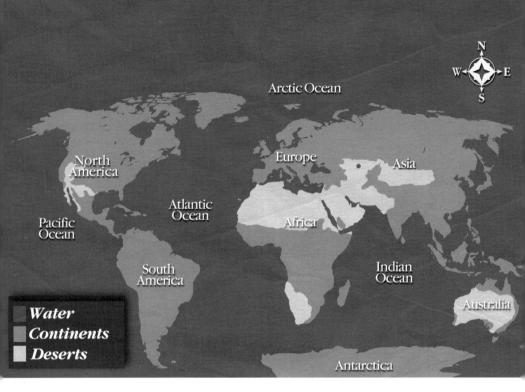

Deserts

A desert is dry land that receives less than 10 inches (25 cm) of rain each year. Deserts cover about one-third of Earth's land.

The Sahara Desert in Africa is the largest desert in the world. It covers more than 3.5 million square miles (9 million sq. km). It is about the size of the United States. The largest desert in North America is the Sonoran Desert in Southern California, Arizona, and northwest Mexico. It covers about 120,000 square miles (310,800 sq. km).

Kinds of Deserts

Each desert looks different. Some are flat. Others have small hills. Some have rocky cliffs.

There are hot and cold deserts. Hot deserts are very warm during the day. The Sahara and the Sonoran are hot deserts. Cold deserts have temperatures below freezing during the day for part of the year. One cold desert is the large Gobi Desert in Mongolia and China. Snow covers the ground there for part of the year.

EVAPORATION

This diagram shows how water is reused in the water cycle.

The Water Cycle

Deserts lose more water through evaporation than they receive in rainfall. Evaporation means the water turns into a gas called water vapor. A gas is a substance that will spread to fill any space that contains it.

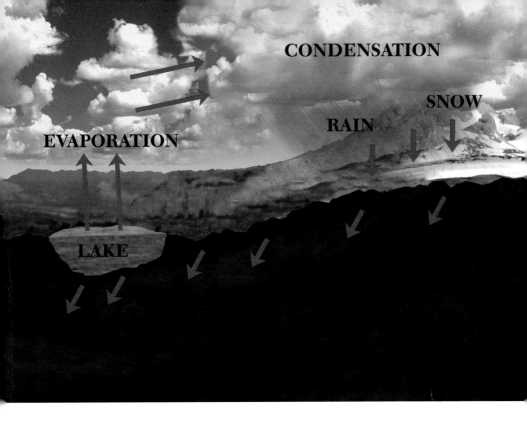

CONDENSATION

EVAPORATION

RAIN

SNOW

LAKE

Earth uses its water again and again in the water cycle. Water from the oceans, lakes, rivers, and streams evaporates. Plant leaves and stems also release water as water vapor.

Water vapor rises into the atmosphere. An atmosphere is a mix of gases around a planet. There, it cools and becomes clouds. It falls back to Earth again as rain or snow. Then the cycle starts over again.

This desert formed because it is near mountains and far from the ocean.

How Deserts Form

Many deserts form around large mountain ranges. Air cools as it travels up a mountain. The cool air forms rain clouds. The air becomes dry as it passes over the mountain after rain falls from the clouds onto the mountain. Since there is little or no rain left for the land around the mountain so deserts form. This is called a rain-shadow effect.

Other deserts form on western coasts of continents. A continent is one of Earth's seven major bodies of land. Places near the coasts receive little rain. That is how deserts form there. Fog that forms over the ocean is often the only source of water for plants. Fog is a cloud that touches the ground.

Deserts also form in other places. Land may become a desert if it is far from an ocean. Deserts form just outside the tropics. The tropics are hot places near the middle of Earth. Dry air goes there from high in the atmosphere. The Australian desert formed for this reason.

Desert soil can be rocky, salty, or sandy. Few kinds of plants can grow in desert soil.

About Deserts

Most deserts have little soil. Some deserts are mainly sand. Sand is very tiny grains of rock. Other deserts have a fine, grayish soil. Still other deserts have small, polished rocks on the surface.

Some desert soils may be full of salt. This is because water that used to be there has dried and left behind the salt it contained. Salt kills most plants. Few plants grow in these salty places.

Some desert soils have many nutrients. Nutrients are things that people, plants, and animals need to stay healthy. But the nutrients need to be broken down in water for plants to use them. Without water, few or no plants grow.

Large areas of sand dunes are called sand seas, or ergs.

Climate

Temperatures in the desert change greatly from day to night. During the day, the Sun warms the ground. Temperatures get very hot. In summer, most hot deserts have temperatures higher than 100° Fahrenheit (38° C) during the day.

At night, the desert temperature drops 30° or more. It often becomes cold. Temperatures in the Sahara Desert rise to 120° Fahrenheit (49° C) during the day in summer. At night in winter, they can drop to around 32° Fahrenheit (0° C).

There is very little rainfall in deserts. Most deserts receive less than 4 inches (10 cm) of rain a year. The driest desert in the world is the Atacama Desert in Chile. Rain did not fall for 400 years in some parts of this desert.

A desert can go for a year or more with no rain. Then a storm will dump several inches of rain all at once. The rain causes floods. Most water evaporates before the ground soaks it up.

Deserts on western coasts often get no rain. But fog blows in from the oceans. The desert's plants and animals use the water in fog to live.

Powerful desert winds often blow soil from place to place. In sandy deserts, wind blows sand into huge hills called **dunes**. Sand dunes can be hundreds of feet high. The blowing wind keeps changing the look of sand dunes.

The saguaro cactus has a thick stem and thick branches. These help it hold in water.

DESERT PLANTS

It is hard for plants to grow in deserts. There is not enough rain, the soil is poor, and it is too hot. But some kinds of plants are adapted to live in deserts. The most common desert plants are small bushes called shrubs. Cacti may also grow in deserts. Cacti are leafless plants with thick stems. Needle-like spines cover cacti instead of leaves.

The saguaro cactus is one of the most common cacti in the United States. It is a large cactus with thick, upward-growing branches. The saguaro grows in the Sonoran Desert.

One common plant in North American deserts is the yucca. Yuccas are evergreen plants with tall, thick stems.

Some creams that people put on their skin are made out of the agave plant.

Evergreens

An evergreen plant keeps its green leaves or needles all year. The Joshua tree is a famous kind of yucca plant. It is one of the tallest desert plants in the United States. A Joshua tree may grow to 40 feet (12 m) or more.

How Plants Adapt

Most desert plants have ways to keep water inside them. Different plants store water in different places. Yucca and cacti store water in their thick stems and branches. Agave and aloe plants store water in their thick leaves.

Water-storing plants soak up as much water as they can when a lot of rain falls. This makes their stems or leaves grow larger. When it is dry, the plants use the water that they have stored. The stems or leaves get smaller as the plants use the water.

Desert plants have fewer **stomata** than plants in other biomes. Stomata are small holes in a plant's leaf. Water escapes through stomata. Some desert plants keep their stomata closed during the day. The heat would make a lot of water leave the plant. The plants open their stomata at night when it is cooler.

Many desert plants also have a thick, waxy coating. This coating seals the plant and helps hold water inside it.

The kangaroo rat digs burrows, or underground holes, to keep cool.

Desert Animals

The desert is home to few large mammals. A mammal is a warm-blooded animal with a backbone. Large mammals need more water and food than they can find in deserts. Some smaller desert mammals are the jackrabbit, kangaroo rat, and fennec fox.

Many reptiles live in the desert. Reptiles are cold-blooded animals. Cold-blooded animals have body temperatures that are about the same as the air or water around them. Common desert reptiles are snakes, lizards, and tortoises. A tortoise is another name for a turtle, especially one that lives on land.

The vulture is a scavenger. It keeps the desert clean by eating the remains of other animals.

Small Creatures

The desert is full of insects, spiders, and scorpions. A scorpion has eight legs and a tail with a stinger on it. Large spiders called tarantulas live in deserts. Common desert insects are beetles and ants.

Some birds that live in deserts are owls, hawks, and vultures. Vultures are scavengers. A scavenger is an animal that eats any dead animals it finds.

How Desert Animals Live

Animals that live in the desert must be able to keep cool during the hot days. Some animals lay in the shade of plants or rocks. But most desert animals dig **burrows**. Burrows are underground holes or tunnels. It is cooler under the ground. Most burrowing desert animals come out only at night when it is cooler outside.

Most desert animals need to find water. Many animals drink from water holes. A water hole is a place where water collects. Many green plants often grow on the land next to water holes. These places with many plants are called **oases**.

Some animals get water by eating water-storing plants. They eat the leaves and stems where water is stored.

Other animals **estivate**. To estivate is to spend the summer in a sleeplike state. Estivating animals become active when it cools in winter.

Animal Adaptations

Animals' bodies have changed over thousands of years to help them live better in deserts. Most animals are light-colored. Light colors do not soak up sunlight. Instead, the sun bounces off the animals. This helps them stay cool.

Most mammals cool off by sweating. To sweat is to give off water through small holes in skin. But many desert animals do not sweat to cool off. They need their water. Instead of sweating, they have extra-large ears with many blood vessels near the surface. Air blows over the blood vessels and cools the animal's blood. The cooler blood flows through the animal and cools the rest of its body. Fennec foxes and jackrabbits cool off this way.

It is hard for animals to walk in the hot sand. Some animals have thick fur on the bottoms of their feet. The fur keeps their feet from getting burned. Other animals have hooves. A hoof is a hard covering on the foot. Camels and desert bighorn sheep have hooves. Fennec foxes have fur on the bottoms of their feet.

> The scales of this blue-tongued lizard help it hold water inside its body.

Some animals have ways to keep water inside their bodies. Waterproof scales cover snakes and lizards. A scale is a flat and thick piece of skin. Scales help keep a reptile from drying up. Other animals can store water. Camels can drink many gallons of water at a time. The water is stored in their bodies.

This man lives in the desert. He is wearing a covering called a turban to protect his head.

DESERTS AND PEOPLE

It is hard for people to live in deserts. To live there, most people must find ways to bring water and food into deserts. Still, a few people have always lived in deserts.

Aborigines live in the Great Australian Desert. Aborigines are native people of Australia. They move from place to place to find water to drink. They eat insects, animals, and plants.

Nomads live in the deserts of Africa and Asia. Nomads are people with no fixed home. They live in tents and raise sheep, goats, and cattle. They move around to find food, water, and grass for their animals.

The fennec fox is well-adapted to desert life. It would be hard for this fox to live elsewhere.

Desert Cities

People today have built cities in some deserts. Pipes bring in water from faraway rivers, lakes, and streams. Farmers use the water to grow crops. People use trucks, ships, and airplanes to bring in food.

Future of Deserts

The desert biome is easily harmed. Many plants and animals there are rare. Rare means there are not many to be found. People driving trucks and other machines can kill tortoises and small desert plants. Other people take cacti from deserts to grow them in their homes.

Many people like the sunshine and warm temperatures found in deserts. They build homes and cities there. The desert plants are removed and animals lose their homes. Lawns and gardens and golf courses take their places.

In other places, new deserts are forming. Some form where people cut down too many trees. Others form where grasslands are being eaten up by too many grazing animals. Grazing animals are grass-eating animals people raise for food. Soil blows away when these animals eat too much grass. There are no longer plants or roots to keep the soil in place.

Most new deserts have little plant or animal life. Some will move in over time. But new deserts are not good homes for the well-adapted plants and animals of old deserts.

GLOSSARY

adapt (uh-DAPT)—to have features that let a living thing fit well in a special place

burrow (BUR-oh)—a hole or tunnel in the ground where an animal lives

climate (KLYE-mit)—the usual weather and weather changes of a place

dune (DOON)—a sand hill

estivate (ESS-ti-vayt)—to rest in a sleeplike state for the summer

nomad (NOH-mad)—a person with no fixed home

oases (oh-AY-sees)—places in the desert where there is water and trees and other plants grow

stomata (stoh-MAH-tah)—tiny holes in a plant's leaf through which water escapes

Internet Sites

DesertUSA 2000
http://www.desertusa.com/index.html

Mysterious Journey—Deserts
http://library.thinkquest.org/26634/featuresf.htm

Useful Addresses

Chihuahuan Desert Research Institute
P.O. Box 1332
Alpine, TX 79831

The Living Desert
47-900 Portola Avenue
Palm Desert, CA 92260

Sonoran Desert State Park
P.O. Box 40427
Tucson, AZ 85717-0427

INDEX